Tibet
in Pictures

Volume 1
Expedition to Central Tibet

Text and Photos by
Li Gotami Govinda

Dharma Publishing

No part of this book, either text or photos, may be
reproduced without written permission from the author and publisher.
For information, address:
Dharma Publishing, 2425 Hillside Avenue,
Berkeley, California 94704 USA

Jacket: Ratnasambhava, from p. 81
Frontispiece: Vairocana, from p. 44

LIBRARY OF CONGRESS CATALOGING IN PUBLICATION DATA

Govinda, Li Gotami.
    Tibet in pictures.

    Bibliography: vol. 2, p. 204
    Includes index.
    CONTENTS: vol. 1. Expedition to central Tibet.—
vol. 2. Expedition to western Tibet.
    1. Tibet—Description and travel—Views. I. Title.
DS786.G67   951'.5'0222   79-21352
ISBN 0-913546-57-7 (v. 1)
ISBN 0-913546-58-5 (v. 2)

Typeset in Fototronic Plantin, printed, and bound by
Dharma Press, Emeryville, California

9 8 7 6 5 4 3 2

To Kiän
(*Lama Anagarika Govinda*)
in undying memory
of our journeys into the
Land of the Thousand Buddhas

Foreword

*In the land of gold,
there are no ordinary stones*

Tibet in Pictures presents photographs of the sacred art, landscape, and people of Tibet, and uniquely places these images in the context of a religious pilgrimage. Li Gotami Govinda approached her subject with a rare combination of devotion and great artistic skill, which allowed her to truly record these images of ancient art and culture. Though the full historical importance of the photographs could not be known at the time they were taken, they are inspired with an artistry that captures, in particular, the fine aesthetic quality of the tenth and eleventh century art of Tsaparang, an important part of Tibet's religious and artistic heritage. Publication of these volumes is a unique opportunity for Dharma Publishing.

Although the memory of Tibet now lives primarily through images and pictures, few pictorial records of Tibetan art and culture are accessible today. Over the past decade, through reproductions of numerous thankas, as well as through translations on various aspects of Tibetan culture and philosophy, Dharma Publishing has been able to give readers a few glimpses of the vast treasurehouse of Tibetan art and culture. We are very grateful to Li Gotami Govinda for contributing the photographs in these volumes to the growing body of knowledge about Tibet in the West.

I hope that as Tibetan art becomes more known in the West, there will be made available extensive commentaries on its nature and meaning. Without such explanation, the figures of the tantric iconography are easily misunderstood as external deities to be worshipped, or as fantastic, even hallucinatory imaginings. This is not, however, the case. In the Tibetan tradition, art is a guide to enlightenment, a system of symbolic images for transforming ordinary, dualistic consciousness into the highest understanding of reality. Ultimately, art is the realization of the infinite beauty of human wisdom.

To appreciate Tibetan art we must appreciate ourselves, the nature of our awareness, and all that is manifested within it.

Tibetan art is a part of the miraculous process of manifestation, not a comment on it or something separate from it. A beautiful creation of the human mind, this art precisely reveals to the contemplating mind its own true nature. By appreciating the beauty of the art, by concentrating on its gestures, forms, proportions, and colors (which exactly correspond to the ways of being they are considered to manifest), it is possible to activate a process of inner development that produces a new dimension of consciousness. As the object of symbolic art introduces us to our true nature, our subjective world is transformed.

Tibetan art guides us to compassion, the greatest human quality. The beauty that is the essence of art invites an understanding that heals our senses and thoughts, and opens our hearts to an ecstatic quality that touches a great love. This then leads us to fuller appreciation of the beauty of art, awakening ever greater dimensions of understanding and compassion, opening a realm of appreciation that can be extended to all appearance. In the unfolding interaction of beauty and love, infinite beauty flows into infinite compassion, the all-inclusive love that has no objects. Art is then completed, made one with the viewer, and existence itself is transformed into perfect art. The reality hidden to ordinary human consciousness is clearly revealed. We discover in the unfolding of appearance, the beauty of art.

Tibetan art can guide us to this realization, but this art is not simply a vehicle to profound knowledge, nor does it exist solely in order to convey it. The knowledge is there because the art is not separate from the reality it brings to our attention. The art, the reality are complete.

Only a few people familiar with Western culture have contributed to the understanding of Tibetan art and culture in the West. I want to thank both Li Gotami Govinda and Lama Govinda personally, and on behalf of Dharma Publishing, for the support they have given to the art, culture, and people of Tibet. The benefits brought about through their influence are greatly appreciated.

Tarthang Tulku
December, 1979

Preface

NĀMO BUDDHĀYA!

During the years 1947–1949, my husband, Lama Anagarika Govinda, and I undertook to make two expeditions (sponsored by *The Illustrated Weekly of India*) into the sacred land of Tibet. The objective of our first journey was to obtain passes (*lamyiks*) from the Dalai Lama, in Central Tibet, to permit us to go to Tsaparang in Western Tibet, and to work there, copying, tracing, photographing, etc., the exquisite works of art and knowledge that stood in the temples built by Lotsawa Rinchen Zangpo in the eleventh century. Lotsawa Rinchen Zangpo was a translator, builder, and scholar who was responsible for many of the temples, religious monuments, and libraries of Western Tibet.

If the *lamyiks* were granted, it meant that, upon adequate payment, we were to be supplied with food and transport, without fail, by the villagers all along the route. This was *very important* in Tibet, because if one did *not* possess *lamyiks*, no one was allowed to sell you food or supply you with caravans of yaks to proceed along the treks—and this situation, of course, could end in a major disaster! Therefore, we first went along the Lhasa Route to Gyantse, to secure these very important *lamyiks* from his Holiness's Tibetan government.

When we got to Gyantse, however, we soon learned that the Dalai Lama was on tour, and might be away for several weeks. This seemed to be very disappointing news, which later on turned out to be a blessing in disguise! Without wasting much time, we went about seeing the town and making mental notes about which things were good for sketching and photographing. That the Monastic City of Gyantse was out and out a real treasurehouse (containing many sacred objects and images we would wish to work on), soon became more than evident. This Monastic City contained the Gyantse Kumbum (The Golden Temple of the Hundred Thousand Images), and several *gompas* (monasteries) full of beautiful statues, frescoes of Buddhas and Bodhisattvas, and beautifully illuminated scriptures and prayer books worth studying and photographing. What more could we have wished for, I wonder?

I decided on photographing the sacred images in the Kumbum and the main temple of Gyantse first, and because the Buddhas willed it so, the Dalai Lama did *not* return soon! I was able to make innumerable sketches, portraits, landscapes, and photographs for the span of more than three months, in the second largest city of Tibet, Gyantse—and beyond.

Of course, the *lamyiks* and the permission to work in Tsaparang were finally granted, and so back to India we had to go, to collect material for the second and main expedition to Tsaparang in Western Tibet. No time was lost, and as soon as possible all necessary things were collected, and we found ourselves in Almora, arranging a caravan to take us once again into Tibet, this time by way of the Lipu Lekh Pass.

After a journey of several months, we reached Tsaparang, our destination. Our arrival was marked quite dramatically by a beautiful rainbow, which was most auspicious, everyone said, because rainbows are very rare in Tibet, and on this occasion, it did not even rain! This was indeed an excellent beginning, I felt.

A few days after our arrival and our first inspection tour, I recall, we set about making a work plan, and it seemed to me that first photographing most of the important statues would be the safest and wisest thing to do. Somehow intuition seemed to tell me that if something were to happen later (in spite of our passes from Lhasa), at least we would have some good photographs to go back with. How right I was, neither my husband nor I knew at the time.

I felt what had to be done *must* be done soon, and so then and there, I decided to once again inspect each and every one of those priceless images and frescoes in the Red and White Temples of Tsaparang, this time very critically. They were all, without exception, I noted, quite exquisite.

At times I was dumb with delight, and stared with wonder at the beautiful forms of Dolma, Chenrezig, and others, with whom we were so very familiar, and before whose images we had spent so many beautiful hours in other temples and sanctuaries of Central, Southern, and Western Tibet. I noticed, too, their exquisite elongated waists (for which the statues of Tsaparang are renowned), and discussed with my husband their place in Tibetan iconography. These images and frescoes seemed to vibrate with life, like living gods; they seemed to be smiling at me now, happy in the knowledge that we had undertaken, successfully, so perilous a journey in order to be with them in person. I felt myself becoming more and more alive to their reality.

They had been great in a former dynasty, when Lotsawa Rinchen Zangpo had built his hundred and eight *stūpas* and had caused these mighty works of art to be fashioned by inspired artists of the eleventh century. Thousands had thronged these very halls, to pay homage to these sacred shrines. They had remained great after the Empire of Guge had been destroyed, and the whole of Tsaparang (its one-time capital) was abandoned in the seventeenth century, six hundred years later. And they were just as glorious today, though the walls of their temples were crumbling to dust. I felt a glow of joy in the realization of the strength and beauty of these ageless masterpieces.

After this second inspection tour, we soon started work, first holding a *pūja* in the Red and White Temples, feeling we had been blessed by the Buddhas and Bodhisattvas with whom we were to live for the next glorious three months. How much work we did in those three fruitful months must be seen to be believed. I can hardly believe it myself: fresco tracings, original sketches, color-cards, copies, writings, translations, and last but not least, the hundreds of photographs which I took (a part of which are shown here).

My small folding Kodak befriended me when, to my utter horror, the expensive reflex camera refused to function in the higher altitudes of Tibet. "When you know your camera and love it like a trusted friend, it will work magic for you," I said to my friend several years later while talking about the expeditions over cups of hot tea. She had just then said to me, "Thank goodness you had so many statues to record—at least, *they* do not move!" But my friend was neither a photographer nor an artist, and did not know my secret, that statues do not move, but the *light on them does*, and to get a *perfect* photograph, one *must* study the *light* first, and everything else afterwards. Indeed, statues are some of the most difficult objects to photograph artistically, especially when they are in ill-lit temple halls, as they had been so often during our expeditions to Central and Western Tibet.

In the temples of Tsaparang, just as in the Kumbum of Gyantse and other temples in Central Tibet, the light was particularly poor, and quickly fading. Every image had to be previously studied and observed as to the exact hour and minute at which it could be best photographed—not only to look like a photograph, but to be a well-composed *picture* as well. Not a single exposure was to be wasted through lack of knowledge about correct timing or the best light effect on the image,

Examining Tibetan scriptures after the expedition

for due to film rationing in India, I had not been able to purchase as many film rolls as an expedition of this sort required. If any exposures were wasted, I could never photograph that particular image or scene again. Therefore, it was a breathless chase from one temple to another, to note the changes the fading light made on those priceless images, during different hours of the day.

I thanked my lucky stars that I had gathered so much knowledge about photography in previous years (when I had been one of the founder-members of the Camera Pictorialists of Bombay), for now, that very knowledge came to my rescue as nothing else could ever have done. If the light had not been too good during the day, I used to mount my camera firmly onto a tripod, open the lens, go away for ten or fifteen minutes, then come back and click it shut! Although I never forgot that the camera's eye sees more in the dark than a human eye can, I did not know, at that time, whether my exposures were correct or not. It was not until we returned to India and developed those film rolls that I realized that indeed I must have been particularly blessed, for not a single exposure of those images and frescoes had come out a failure.

For my readers, who may not be familiar with Buddhist art and Tibet in general, I have written short notes next to each picture, to explain what each photograph is trying to convey. Tibetan words have been rendered phonetically, so that they can be easily pronounced; the Sanskrit has been transliterated according to the standard system. Should further information be required, especially in regard to the sacred images here pictured, my husband's books, *Foundations of Tibetan Mysticism* and *The Way of the White Clouds*, may be consulted.

My sincere thanks, firstly, to all Buddhas and Bodhisattvas, for their gift of continuous inspiration. I am also greatly indebted to Mrs. Chester Carlson of Rochester, to Werner Erhard of The *est* Foundation, to the German branch of the 'Arya Maitreya Mandala', to the Green Gulch Zen Center, to the publisher and printer of these books, and lastly, to all those who, in so many small ways, have made it possible for me to pass on to the world in general a few of these last records of some of the most glorious works of Buddhist art, which are now, alas, no more in Tsaparang, nor in the other temples and sanctuaries of that sacred Tibet which we were privileged to visit.

Li Gotami Govinda
August, 1979

Introduction

By Lama Anagarika Govinda

This work is not only a collection of beautiful pictures, but has the unique distinction of bringing to the notice of the world the last documentary records of a vanishing culture. Tibet's was a great and ancient civilization which flourished with unbroken vitality for more than a millenium, right up to our time, when it met with almost total destruction by the conquering hordes of a fanatical enemy who not only conquered and occupied the country, but did his best to annihilate the last traces of its culture, its religion, its art, and even its ethnographic identity. And this happened exactly at the moment when for the first time in the history of this planet, humanity was on the verge of becoming conscious of its essential oneness and its future common fate.

In this century, science and technology made possible for the first time the establishment of effective and instantaneous communication among all nations in all parts of the globe, but the voice of Tibet was too weak to be heard amid the babel of voices, the contending interests and ambitions of the stronger nations. Thus has been lost the great chance to preserve the last living link with the most ancient traditions of humanity, traditions which the geographical and cultural isolation of Tibet had preserved in their purity.

It is only now, with the enlarged horizons of modern science and psychology, that we begin to understand that the unity of humanity does not depend only on the breaking down of geographical barriers and obstructions in the form of oceans and insurmountable mountains, barriers of space; but also on the overcoming of the barriers of time between the past and the present, barriers which prevent us from communicating or re-establishing contact with our past.

This is why we are now trying to piece together the history of life on this planet, to trace the awakening of consciousness from the simplest to the most differentiated organisms, to trace the paths from the origin of man to the emergence of various civilizations, to the creation of art and religion, philosophy and science, social organizations and the technical skills that have led to man's mastery over nature—except his own.

And here we come to the problem of our time: we have learned to master the forces of nature, but we have not yet achieved mastery over ourselves, our inner life, our psychic and spiritual forces, in short, the dormant faculties of our deeper consciousness, which after all created the world in which we live and all that we have achieved in the form of manifold civilizations. These faculties permit us to see the fundamental oneness of life, the interrelatedness of all peoples and civilizations and the ultimate oneness of humanity; they even allow us our conquest over the forces of nature. Yet we do not understand these faculties.

Tibet had chosen to go a different way: to renounce the conquest of the forces of nature (as it had renounced the conquest of neighboring countries, which it was about to achieve when Buddhism took possession of Tibet). Instead she chose to cultivate and develop the powers of inner perception, which are the very source of all human culture, knowledge, and achievement. Unless man is able to coordinate, unify, and ultimately integrate these powers within himself and thereby become complete, how can he expect to create a harmonious and united human world? This was the way the Tibetans viewed the problem of the future of humanity, a problem that now faces us on a global scale.

Surrounded by powerful neighbors, but protected by mighty mountain ranges and extreme climatic conditions that acted as a sufficiently strong deterrent to invasions during the past, Tibet had not built up military defenses, but had concentrated its energies entirely on the pursuit of its cultural and religious life and the simple necessities of its self-contained economy. Thus it became an easy prey to the vastly superior weapons of modern military power and organization. When the Chinese Communists invaded Tibet, they succeeded in completely wiping out Tibet's thousand-year-old culture by prohibiting all religious activity, converting monasteries into military barracks, destroying temples and images, and forcing the surviving monks into labor-camps.

The world has been a shocked, though powerless, witness of this tragedy; but at the same time, something in the consciousness (and perhaps even in the conscience) of the world has been stirred, if not awakened. We begin to realize that Tibet attempted a most remarkable and courageous spiritual exploration, not simply a matter of metaphysical speculation, but a practical investigation of the human mind and depth-consciousness which was unique in the history of mankind. This was an attempt to align life with a great cosmic vision that embraced both the material and the spiritual aspects of man and his world, and was capable of transforming both through the power of creative imagination. It was a vision based on the oneness of life and the universality of consciousness, a vision which gave meaning to man's existence and provided each individual with an aim worth striving for: the realization of this vision.

Each of the great civilizations of the past has made an attempt to formulate, to express from the deepest recesses of our consciousness (nowadays inadequately called 'the Unconscious') a particular attitude or dimension of the human mind. No single civilization was perfect in itself or could provide a total solution to the human problem; circumstances and the conditions of life always change. Yet each of them contributed a valuable step towards the solution, an experience which enriched and deepened the human mind. This enrichment took the form of a cultural heritage that survived the greatest and most powerful empires, their triumphs and conquests, their wealth and material achievements, and their final defeats and dissolution. What is left of these civilizations in the consciousness of the world and continues to be of lasting influence and inspiration to countless later generations are the fragile works of those who had no worldly power or possessions: the works of artists, poets, seers, and thinkers, those who lived in the shadow of the mighty and powerful, and gave shape and expression to the dreams of man, to his religious aspirations, his deepest feelings, his faith in the meaning of life and in the laws of the universe upon which his life was based. It is this, our common heritage, which guarantees the continuity of human culture in any new form of civilization.

If, as all signs of our time seem to indicate, we stand at the threshold of a new world, then we have all the more reason to look back upon the path we have traversed, not in order to revive the past, but in order to understand our present situation and the possibilities and direction of our future, which can have a meaning only in relationship to the past that is living within us and has formed us into what we are. The past contains both our origin and our aim.

Tibet's was the last surviving civilization in which the oldest traditions of humanity were still alive, enshrined in the ancient Nyingma traditions. The religious and intellectual culture that had ripened in India during more than a millenium of Buddhist history had been transformed and elevated within Tibetan culture to its highest level. Because of this rare combination of factors, the preservation of the unique artistic, religious, literary, philosophical, and psychological achievements of Tibet is our most urgent task.

Tibetan art, of which the Western world is only now beginning to be aware, offers more than aesthetic pleasure, for it is based not merely on a pantheon of mythological gods and deified saints, but on experiences of meditation that are a rich treasure of archetypal symbols. These symbols reveal some of the deepest mysteries of the human mind and provide the key to many of the problems of modern depth-psychology. Most of the images described in iconographical works are not deities existing as separate entities, but are conscious projections of meditative experience, as described in the respective *sādhana* texts (or practice instructions).

No iconography can have any meaning without the knowledge of these texts and their practical application within the living tradition, which soon may die out. Never has the world witnessed anything comparable to the speed and suddenness with which a great and long-established civilization was erased from the face of the earth; and at the same time, never was the opportunity to preserve its heritage greater than it is in this our time, when we have both the presence of those who still embody the living tradition of Tibet, and the technical means to reproduce and record through word and picture, in audible and visible form, all aspects of Tibetan life, art, and literature.

The photographs reproduced in this work make a particularly valuable contribution to our knowledge and remembrance of Tibet. They not only show the country and its people as they were before the Chinese invasion, but they also show a number of Tibet's great works of art that have been unknown to the West. Since many of these works have probably now been destroyed, either by intention or by neglect, the reproductions in these volumes are likely to be the only existing records of these remarkable works of ancient Tibetan art. These photographs were taken by Li Gotami, my wife, during our two-year expedition to Central and Western Tibet, from 1947–49.

The main subject of this expedition was the exploration of the ruined city of Tsaparang, the ancient seat of the Kings of Guge, who ruled Western Tibet after the fall of Lhasa. In Lhasa, the last of the rightful kings of Central Tibet had been murdered by Langdarma, who tried to re-establish the power of the ancient Bonpo faith by destroying Buddhist temples and monasteries, killing their inmates, and persecuting their supporters. Though he himself was overthrown in 842 A.D., after a few years of terror and tyranny, Buddhism had been practically annihilated in Central Tibet. Even after the revival of Buddhism by the six men of Ü and Tsang, who brought back the sacred teachings, Lhasa did not regain its importance until the beginning of the fifteenth century. At that time, Tsongkhapa, the founder of the Gelugpa sect, made it the main seat of his new movement.

In the meantime, however, Western Tibet became the center of Buddhist culture. It was here in the first half of the eleventh century that Tibetan art reached its climax. Here important Buddhist scriptures were translated into classical Tibetan and from here a new wave of Buddhist learning and literature spread over the whole of Tibet. Under the guidance of great scholars of India and Tibet, and under the patronage of generous and pious kings who, in the tenth and eleventh centuries, extended their rule over the whole of Western Tibet, this was an age of tremendous spiritual regeneration and creativity in all fields of knowledge and art. The revival and re-establishment of Buddhism was, in the eyes of these kings, worth the greatest sacrifice and of greater importance than political power. Thus the eleventh century became a golden age of Tibetan Buddhism, a time of birth for the many spiritual movements that gave substance and nourishment to the religious life of a millenium of Tibetan history. The highlight of this glorious epoch was the great Buddhist Council of Tholing, which took place in the famous Golden Temple of Tholing in the middle of the eleventh century. This was the age of Rinchen Zangpo and Atīśa, of Khon Konchog Gyalpo, Bromston, Marpa, and Milarepa and of the schools founded by them: the Kadampas, the Sakyapas, and the Kargyudpas.

Atīśa, one of the greatest scholars of Buddhism in India, was invited to Tholing by the ruling king and took up residence in the Tholing monastery for several years. He had been the head of the great Indian monastic university of Vikramaśīla and was recognized as the highest religious authority by all Buddhists in India. He was as learned as he was pious, and soon his teachings were recognized by all schools of Tibet. His chief disciple, Bromston (born in 1002), founded the Kadampa School, known for its strict monastic discipline and ritual as well as for its meditative practice. It was out of this school that the Gelugpas developed at the end of the fourteenth century under the inspiring leadership and guidance of Tsongkhapa (1357–1419).

Rinchen Zangpo was as great an artist and builder as he was a scholar and translator of Buddhist Sanskrit scriptures into his native Tibetan. Not only the famous monastery and the Golden Temple of Tholing, but also the temples of Tsaparang and many other monasteries and religious monuments all over Western Tibet and Ladakh were created by Rinchen Zangpo. The magnificence of their statues and frescoes has never been surpassed in the history of Tibet. These works set an example and created a style that dominated the most fruitful period of Tibetan art. In contrast to the more or less stereotyped Buddha images of Chinese and Central Asian origin, of which those of the temple of Iwang in South Tibet are a typical example, the statues of Tsaparang combined the almost abstract plastic qualities of great sculpture with an intense inner life, a life which seems to be more real than that of the average human being.

That this living quality has been caught in the photographs is due to the patient and reverential attitude with which Li Gotami approached and observed these statues and frescoes during our three-months stay in the deserted ruins of Tsaparang. The light in the big temple hall mainly depended on the reflections of sunlight that entered through an opening in the roof, and fell upon the golden shoulder of the main image in the apsis of the temple. With the movement of the sun, the reflected light traveled from one part of the temple hall to the other, so that each of the statues and frescoes received its best light during only a very short period of each day. Careful study of the effects of light and shadow on each of these over-lifesize statues was necessary in order to take photographs which not only gave a factually faithful picture, but also revealed the living spirit embodied in each of these inspired works of art.

During our long stay and work under the eyes and in the mysterious presence of these awe-inspiring statues and their frescoed surroundings, we became more and more aware of their spiritual vitality, created by the combined forces of devotion, concentration, and vision. We felt their presence like that of living beings who surrounded us in the great stillness and eerie solitude of the abandoned city. Like powerful friends, they gave us the strength and the courage to endure the hardships of cold, hunger, and the difficulties of a life that had been reduced to the sheerest necessities for survival.

The knowledge that we were perhaps the last people to see and appreciate these great works of religious art, the knowledge of our trust to convey their beauty and message to the world at large, made us forget all hardships and kept us in a state of inspired activity. Thus we were able to make exact tracings and color notes of several hundred fresco panels. These we brought back, together with samples of fragments which had fallen off damaged frescoes. A complete set of thirty-two panels depicting the life of Buddha Śākyamuni was traced by Li Gotami. Three of these panels, executed in their original colors, are now the property of the Prince of Wales Museum in Bombay, where they occupy a central place in the Tibetan section.

Though we had no inkling of the magnitude of the disaster that was to befall Tibet, we were conscious of the dark clouds gathering over Tibet's eastern horizon. Our concern, however, was primarily directed toward the precarious state of those crumbling temples and their priceless treasures, the frescoes and images that would hardly survive our generation, unless something were done for their preservation. It never occurred to us then, that not merely neglect, but willful destruction as well would make an end to these last remnants of a great age. How swiftly this destruction could take place was demonstrated by the fate of the Kumbum of Gyantse, the Temple of the Hundred Thousand Images, which according to recent reports, was destroyed during the so-called Cultural Revolution that rocked the whole of China and was carried into Tibet.

The Kumbum was a great encyclopedia of Tibetan iconography in sculpture and frescoes that rose as a nine-storied Pagoda-Temple in the walled monastic town of Gyantse. There were about eighty chapels rising in tiers like cells in a beehive, and each of these sanctuaries contained a number of exquisite statues, from about life-size to two-storied giant Buddhas. Some of the most beautiful statues of the fourteenth century Kumbum still showed some influence of the

classical period of Western Tibetan art, though the elongated waists which gave such dignity to the images of Tsaparang (strangely reminiscent of a similar tendency in Gothic sculpture) were no more in evidence. In addition to the many statues, each of the walls within these shrines was covered from top to bottom with the most minutely executed frescoes of superb workmanship.

From an architectural point of view, the Kumbum was one of the most remarkable buildings in Tibet. It combined the characteristics of a *chorten*—a symbolic monument derived from the early Indian *stūpa*, a tumulus-like structure in which the relics of the historical Buddha originally were enshrined —with those of a temple dedicated to innumerable forms of Buddhas, Bodhisattvas, saints and saviors, demonical and divine figures of all kinds. Each of the eighty separate chapels was dedicated to a particular aspect of Buddha- or Bodhisattvahood and had its own particular form of worship and meditative practice (*sādhana*). The latter found its symbolic expression in the mandala, which shows the concentric approach towards the central principle, represented by a divine figure and surrounded by its emanations and attributes of power, arranged according to their relationship to the center as well as to their mutual interdependence. Thus each of the chapels of the Kumbum represented a complete mandala of spiritual emanations or visionary experiences of meditation. In the four big chapels in the round central structure of the Kumbum, the wall space was big enough to show actual mandalas, filled with thousands of figures, each of which symbolized or corresponded to a certain meditative experience or state of consciousness.

Mandalas on the highest level represent the totality of the human consciousness, a spiritual cosmos, a replica of the universe. The word 'mandala' literally means 'circle', but in religious parlance it designates a concentric arrangement of interrelated symbols, pertaining to experiences of meditation and religious practice. There are abstract mandalas, consisting either of purely geometrical diagrams, or of diagrams inscribed with single letters, syllables, or sacred formulas (mantras). Each of these letters, syllables, and formulas represents a particular aspect of psychic force or spiritual power, through which the human mind calls up the symbols of a higher reality in which it participates.

A second type of mandala is that in which the written

symbols or formulas are replaced by ritual emblems, associated with various aspects of spiritual power, as codified in iconography. The third and most intricate type of mandala contains pictorial representations of enlightened beings, such as Buddhas, Bodhisattvas, divine protectors in human and non-human forms, in different gestures (*mudrās*) and colors, accompanied by symbolic animals and surrounded by various types of halos or flames.

While the mandalas mentioned so far are usually two-dimensional, i.e. in the form of frescoes, painted scrolls (*thankas*), or xylographs, there are also three-dimensional mandalas with plastic representations of Buddhas and their emanations and retinues, in short, the whole pantheon of beings, inhabiting this and the other worlds of the spiritual universe. And finally, there are abstract three-dimensional mandalas in the form of monumental architecture, of which the Kumbum was an outstanding example. Not only was each chapel of the Kumbum constructed as a mandala, but the entire Kumbum itself was a monumental three-dimensional mandala.

The main architectural features of the Kumbum, as in all developed forms of the *stūpa* or *chorten*, symbolize the fundamental elements of the universe:

1. the state of solidity is represented by the cubic forms of the substructure, namely the four rectangular terraces;

2. the state of fluidity is represented by the round drum-shaped middle structure which is likened to a water-pot or vase (Tibetan: *bum-pa*);

3. the state of incandescence or the fiery state is represented by the conical form of the spire, emerging from the drum-shaped middle structure;

4. the gaseous state is represented by the umbrellalike structure on top of the conical spire;

5. the ethereal state of radiation, interpenetration (symbolizing integration, unification, etc.) is represented by a flaming jewel on top of the umbrella.

In other words, the Kumbum, like all other *chortens*, is a replica of the universe, represented through the five elements of ancient cosmology: earth, water, fire, air, and ether (or space). These 'elements' were conceived not merely as different states of density or aggregation in a material or constantly materializing and dematerializing universe, but also as spiritual forces operating in the psychic centers (chakras) of the human body and the human mind. In accordance with this, the drum- or potlike central structure of the *chorten* represents not only the elementary state of fluidity, but also its spiritual counterpart, the vessel with the 'water of life', the 'Elixir of Immortality'. This vessel with the 'Elixir of Immortality' (Sanskrit: *amṛta-kalaśa*) is the emblem of the Buddha of Infinite Life, the active reflex of Buddha Amitābha, the Buddha of Infinite Light, whose human manifestation was the Enlightened One of our world era, Buddha Śākyamuni. These Buddhas, therefore, occupy the main places, and determine the nature of the mandala as much as the *amṛta-kalaśa*, the central structure of the architecture, determines the character of the *chorten*.

The devotee is expected to contemplate this gigantic mandala as a symbolic representation of the universe, and as a visible formulation of the sacred path which leads to enlightenment, and which can be realized only by one who treads it. Just as one who is about to set out on a big journey first prepares himself by mentally surveying the intended route on a map, so the devotee mentally and physically enters the sacred precincts of the three-dimensional mandala of the *chorten*-temple, and while ascending from plane to plane and circumambulating terrace after terrace and story after story, he brings before his mind's eye the various steps of realization.

With each step, he is reminded by the images of countless Buddhas, Bodhisattvas, Saints, and Sages of the innumerable enlightened beings who trod this path before him and whose spiritual forces are helping and inspiring him in his own effort. Each of these Enlightened Ones reveals his own particular method and achievement, proving that there are as many aspects of the Path as there are living beings, and that there are infinite possibilities of realization.

Thus, sanctuary after sanctuary opens before him, shrine after shrine, temple after temple, each of them forming a mandala within the great mandala, a world within a greater world. Each shrine and each temple is a revelation of a new spiritual world in which the Buddha-Dharma is reflected in its unfathomable profoundness. With each story the devotee ascends a higher plane of intuitive vision, until he reaches the last one, where all diversity disappears and he is confronted with the ultimate integration of Wisdom and Compassion, Mind and Heart, Feeling and Knowledge, in the symbol of Vajradhara, the Adi-Buddha, the primordial Buddha who resides in the very center and depth of our being. Here we reach the source from which every Buddha draws his inspiration and with which he is identified in his ultimate *parinirvāṇa*.

To see all the wonders of the Kumbum, even a few weeks or months would not have been sufficient; to study them in detail would have required years. But all this now belongs to the past, to the irretrievable past, except for a few rare records, like the excellent photographs of this work, which may give at least an inkling of the treasures of art and iconography that were contained in this unique building. The quality of the photographs is all the more remarkable, as modern equipment and facilities were not available at the outset of our expedition in the summer of 1947. Color films were unobtainable in India and even ordinary films were scarce and rationed. Li Gotami had to buy up whatever came her way, and make the best of it, without wasting a single exposure. Her big focal plane reflex camera went out of order and she had to fall back on her small folding Kodak No. 3 taken as an extra. Neither flashlight nor light-meters were at her disposal, so that she had to rely entirely on her own judgment, which fortunately was fortified by many years of experience gathered as one of the founder-members of the Camera Pictorialists of Bombay and as an Associate of the Royal Photographic Society of Great Britain.

However, even greater than these qualifications and her technical skill, was her sincere and genuine devotion to the task she had set herself to accomplish and the indomitable courage with which she faced the hardships and dangers of an expedition into remote regions of the Tibetan highland. Not only did the inclemencies of harsh Tibetan winters present a risk to life and health, but the region at that time (due to political unrest and the uncertainty of Tibet's future in the context of a changing world) was infested by brigands and hostile tribesmen.

It is with gratitude for Li Gotami's brilliant work in both art and photography that these beautiful and historically important volumes are being presented to all lovers of art and human culture. May this work contribute to the understanding and goodwill among men of different races, creeds, and traditions, helping us all to realize the importance of every cultural contribution, past or present, by which humanity is enriched and made conscious of a common heritage and a common future.

Tibet in Pictures

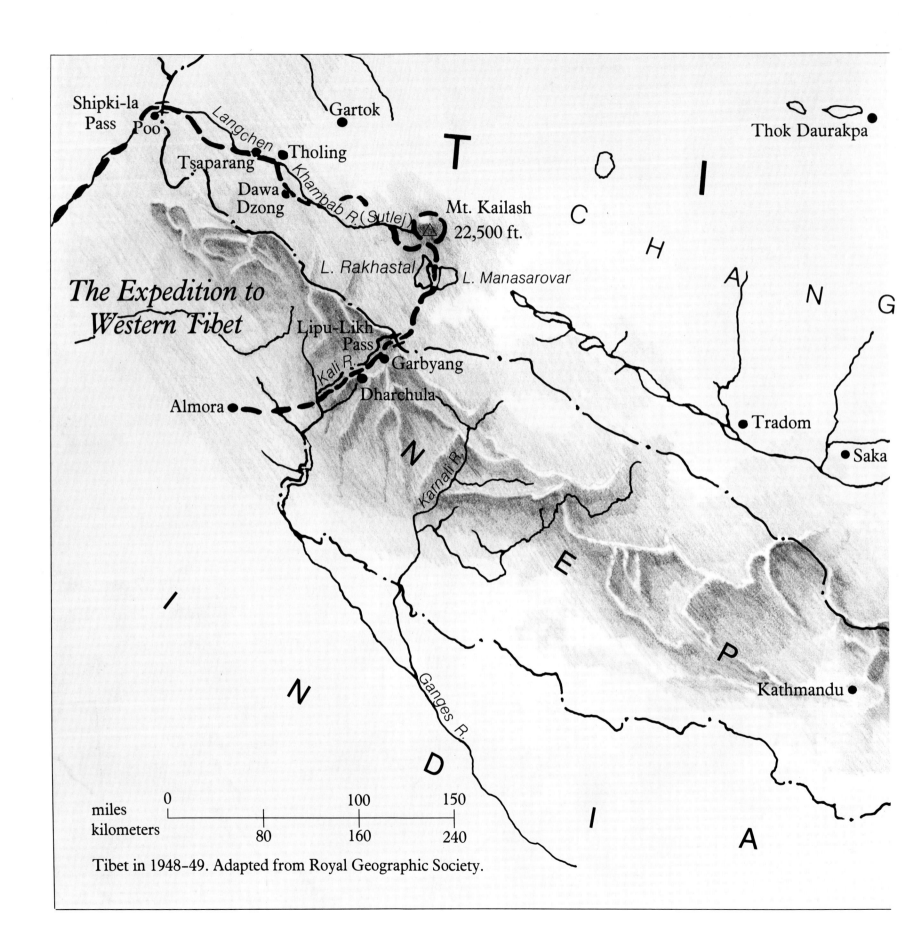

Shipki-la
Pass
Poo

Langchen

Gartok

Khambab R. (Sutlej)

Tholing

Tsaparang

Dawa
Dzong

Mt. Kailash
22,500 ft.

*The Expedition to
Western Tibet*

L. Rakhastal

L. Manasarovar

T

C

H

A

N

G

I

Thok Daurakpa

Lipu-Likh
Pass

Kali R.

Garbyang

Almora

Dharchula

N

Tradom

Saka

Karnali R.

E

N

P

Ganges R.

I

N

D

I

A

Kathmandu

miles
kilometers

0   100   150

80   160   240

Tibet in 1948-49. Adapted from Royal Geographic Society.

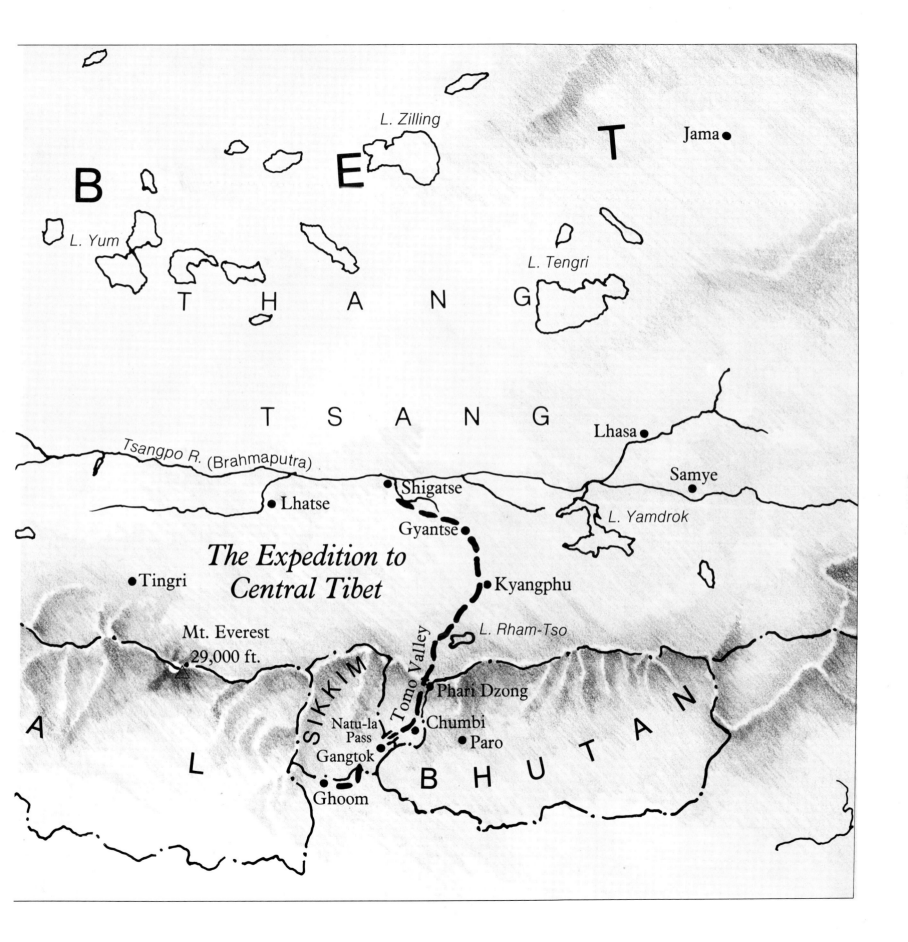

B

E

T

Jama●

L. Zilling

L. Yum

T   H   A   N   G

L. Tengri

T S A N G

Lhasa●

Tsangpo R. (Brahmaputra)

Samye●

●Lhatse

●Shigatse

L. Yamdrok

Gyantse●

The Expedition to Central Tibet

●Kyangphu

●Tingri

L. Rham-Tso

Mt. Everest
29,000 ft.

Phari Dzong●

SIKKIM

Natu-la
Pass

Tomo Valley

Chumbi●

A

Gangtok●

●Paro

L

B H U T A N

●Ghoom

CHANGU-TSO, THE SACRED GREEN LAKE
Sikkim

Silent and still lies the beautiful Changu-Tso, to prepare one's spirit for the long journey into the land of past mysteries, 'The Land of the Thousand Buddhas'. This sacred Green Lake lies at the end of the last stage before crossing the Natu-la Pass into Tibet. It is at an altitude of twelve thousand feet above sea level.

4

CHAMPITHANG
Southern Tibet

Champithang is the first stop over the Natu-la Pass on the sacred soil of Tibet. Forests grow here, for the altitude is lower than in most of Tibet. The wood is used for building, and for heating generous pots of steaming *soecha* (Tibetan buttered tea). Tibetans brew tea in their own manner, generally churning it with yak butter, salt, and soda, and serving it as a light, nourishing broth. How comforting was that first cup of hot *soecha* at Champithang!

AJOREPA RIMPOCHE'S COTTAGE
Tse Choling Monastery,
Southern Tibet

Great lamas do not always live in great
houses! Our Guru's unobtrusive little
dwelling stood at a short distance from
the main temple of Tse Choling Monastery, above the Chumbi Valley, in
Southern Tibet. The tall, coniferous
trees, high hills, and rolling clouds and
mists made the landscape appear like a
Chinese painting. This monastic com-
munity of the Kargyudpa sect contained
many little houses, located around the
central buildings, in which both indi-
viduals and families lived, according to
their own style.

Ajorepa Rimpoche Near Initiation Altar
Tse Choling Monastery

This lama was a Master of Meditation of the Kargyudpa Order, and a follower of Milarepa, the poet-saint of Tibet. Those who follow the path of Milarepa wear robes made of white cotton, for according to their tradition, neither wool nor silk, nor any other kind of material may be worn. The white cotton signifies that its wearer is not a monk and is therefore not bound by monastic rules. In the cold Tibetan climate, the cotton fabric is also a sign of certain powers, namely the ability to generate the intense inner heat called *tumo*. Among the symbolical offerings of water, lights, incense, and so on, are *torma* cones made of roasted barley-flour and butter, and brightly decorated with flowers made from colored butter or discs of paper and cardboard.

Ajorepa Rimpoche
Tse Choling Monastery

Ajorepa Rimpoche was an incarnated *siddha*, one of the perfected ones who lived in India primarily from the sixth to the tenth centuries. The *siddhās* did not live as monks, but as wandering ascetics. Like most of the *siddhās*, this lama, too, never cut his hair, and wore it in long coils, wound around his head. The woven band across his shoulder is used for supporting the knee during long meditations; the white earrings are of conch. *Repa*, which means 'cotton-clad', is a title given to those who follow the path of Milarepa.

8

YOUNG INCARNATE LAMA
Tse Choling Monastery

This little boy is the reincarnated teacher of the aged Ajorepa Rimpoche. He stayed at the same monastery as the aged abbot, and officiated at all religious ceremonies. He was also recognized as being a *tulku* (reincarnation) of Saraha, the Indian *siddha*. During our stay there, he was undergoing strict training in *tumo*, a practice that generates psychic heat.

9

AJOREPA RIMPOCHE'S SON
Tse Choling Monastery

This young boy had been in *tsang-khang* (solitary meditation retreat) for over a year, and had come out just before our arrival at Tse Choling Monastery. It was customary for followers of this order (the Kargyudpas) to go on retreat for long periods that might extend to one, three, six, and sometimes even to nine or twelve years. A small celebration had taken place to mark the end of the boy's retreat, and he was dressed in festive clothes made of silk brocade called *cozen*.

AT THE FOOT OF THE MASTER
*Ajorepa Rimpoche with Li Gotami,
Tse Choling Monastery*

We are sitting in the sun on the verandah outside Tse Choling Monastery.
In his hands, Ajorepa Rimpoche holds
his rosary or prayer beads, which are
used for reciting mantras The prayer
beads are usually one hundred and
eight in number, representing the sacred numbers nine and twelve. (Nine
is the highest single number, and twelve
the number of the Zodiac.) The beads
are very often made from seeds, which
are called *bodhi-tse*. It is a popular belief
that saying mantras with *bodhi-tse* ro-
saries spreads and increases the benefits
of the mantras, like casting seeds on the
ground.

11

STAG DANCE
Tse Choling Monastery

This dance represents a certain religious story that is enacted in a great many temples in Tibet. Pursued by a hunter, a stag takes refuge in the home of a holy man. When the hunter arrives at his door, the holy man explains to him the true consequences of killing. Seeing the truth, the hunter vows to give up hunting, and the stag goes free. The heavy silk and brocade costumes are richly woven with gold and colored threads. The brightly painted masks are meticulously finished in every detail.

Tibetan Dance Mask
Tse Choling Monastery

This papier-mâché mask was made from daphne-bark paper and painted all over with bright colors. The costume was made of rich brocade and appliqué-work, and bound with silk piping. As he danced, the dancer peered through the open mouth of the stag. His movements had a fantastic grace.

TEMPLE DANCERS
Tse Choling Monastery

These dancers represent the Black Hat sect magicians during exorcising ceremonies held at least once a year at most important temples in Tibet. A great many dancers took part in this very effective ceremony. To symbolize the ego, which misleads people into believing that they are permanent and separate beings, a small figure was made of *tsampa* (roasted barley-flour). During the dance, the dancers stabbed this figure of evil several times with daggers. The aprons bear the face of Mahākāla, one of the fearful protectors of the Buddhist faith. The Black Hats originated in pre-Buddhist tradition, and were probably derived from the ancient Bon magicians.

Oṃ Maṇi Padme Hūm
Tomo Valley, Southern Tibet

Oṃ Maṇi Padme Hūm is the mantra of Avalokiteśvara, the patron saint of Tibet (called Chenrezig by Tibetans). One sees this mantra carved and painted on thousands of places in Tibet—on rocks, mountainsides, arches, gateways, 'maniwalls', and on innumerable other places. The mantra welcomes pilgrims, and reminds passers-by of the sacred teachings of the Buddhas. Lama Govinda stands at the foot of the rock inscription.

RELIQUARY OF
TOMO GESHE RIMPOCHE
Dungkar Gompa, Southern Tibet

This silver reliquary of the Great Abbot, Tomo Geshe Rimpoche of Dungkar Gompa, is in the form of a *chorten*
or *stūpa*. It stands two stories high, and
is fashioned in pure silver encrusted
with gold, gems, and dozens of *khows*
(charm-boxes), rings, and other jewelry
donated by his devotees. The monument contains the embalmed body of
the Rimpoche and the religious objects
used by him during his lifetime. Each
khata or scarf thrown over it signifies
a garland of flowers. In the highlands
of Tibet, where flowers and trees are
rare, these *khatas* are used as offerings
of reverence and devotion.

16

THE SEAT OF
TOMO GESHE RIMPOCHE
Dungkar Gompa

In Tibet no one may occupy the seat of a Grand Abbot of a monastery except his *tulku* (recognized reincarnation). After the death of the former Tomo Geshe Rimpoche (Ngawang Kalzang), this seat stood unoccupied at Dungkar Gompa for almost four years, until the *tulku* was found. The folded clothes of the Rimpoche rest on the seat. Sengey Karmo, the white lioness with the green mane (the heraldic sign of Tibet), is shown on the base of the seat. Sengey Karmo was believed to have fed Tomo Geshe Rimpoche during his years of solitary meditation in a cave, high up in the mountains.

DECORATIVE OFFERINGS AT THE GREAT PRAYER FESTIVAL
Dungkar Gompa

The Great Prayer Festival takes place in the first week of every Tibetan New Year. The immense, appliqué-work temple banner is hung from the roof, two stories high, and reaches to the ground below. It represents the historical Buddha Śākyamuni with his two main disciples on either side of him. In front of this temple banner is erected an altar, which is decorated with designs molded from hard butter, gaily painted in bright colors, and mounted on light wooden frames. Dragons and floral designs are common, as well as representations of the Seven Best Things (the ideal Wife, the ideal Householder, the ideal Wheel, the ideal Jewel, the ideal Elephant, the ideal Horse, and the ideal Warrior). At this function, a Tibetan Hobby-Horse Play was enacted, much to the amusement of the audience of hundreds of people from neighboring villages. In larger monasteries, these festivals lasted for several days and nights.

BUDDHA MAITREYA
Dungkar Gompa

Maitreya is the Buddha of the coming age. According to the scriptures, he resides in the Tuṣita Heaven, waiting for the time when he can appear on earth. He symbolizes love for all sentient beings, and is therefore called 'The Loving One'. The statue depicted here is the central image of the temple of Dungkar Gompa, the main seat of the former Tomo Geshe Rimpoche (Ngawang Kalzang). Tomo Geshe Rimpoche especially emphasized the advent of Maitreya, and erected statues of him in all of his monasteries.

ABBOT OF DUNGKAR READING THE SCRIPTURES
Dungkar Gompa

While on a pilgrimage at Chorten Nyima, the former Tomo Geshe Rimpoche (Ngawang Kalzang) had a vision, which was also seen by many others who accompanied him on that pilgrimage. This miraculous event was depicted in a fresco on the wall of one of his rooms. At the time of our visit, Lobonla, the Abbot of Dungkar Gompa, was the only survivor who was present at that event. He then used this room with the fresco on the wall as part of his living quarters.

ABBOT OF DUNGKAR GOMPA
PERFORMING PŪJA
Dungkar Gompa

A *pūja* is a ceremony of devotion that was performed daily without exception at all monasteries and temples. On the low table in front of the abbot are various objects used in the *pūja*. In his hands he holds a *ghaṇṭa* (Bell), which symbolizes awakened wisdom, and a *vajra* (Diamond Scepter), which symbolizes the power to actively realize the means of compassion. Wisdom that is not put into action is without true value; therefore, *ghaṇṭa* and *vajra* must act together.

21

THE ORACLE OF DUNGKAR GOMPA IN ACTION
Dungkar Gompa

The Oracle Priest goes into a trance and is seized by six ancient spirits (or local gods of the country), one after another. These pre-Buddhist local deities were converted into Protectors of the Faith by Padmasambhava, in the eighth century, and became known as guardians of the country. They speak through the mouth of the Oracle Priest during his trance, foretelling important events, and giving advice when important questions are put to them. In this picture the priest sits on a golden throne, clad in gold brocade robes, wearing on his head a magnificent crown with the all-seeing spiritual eye, and on his chest the 'Magic Mirror of Truth'. On a wooden stand to his side rest implements belonging to each of the six spirits. To signify which spirit has seized him, the priest takes hold of the particular implement belonging to that spirit. Here he holds a sword. The Dungkar Gompa Oracle Priest is the only one who is seized by six spirits. Buddhism always respected the local deities and incorporated them into its pantheon. Oracles, however, are confined to the Gelugpa sect.

THE ORACLE PRIEST OF DUNGKAR
Dungkar Gompa

The Oracle of Dungkar Gompa appears in two different forms: threatening and fearful, or peaceful and benevolent. In the latter form he is clad in the robes of a lama. Before him on the table are the sacred objects used during the ceremony of the Transference of Power (*wangkur*) or the giving of blessings. In this ceremony, monks are initiated into certain tantric teachings.

YAMA RĀJA (LORD OF DEATH)
Dungkar Gompa

This is a painted rock-image of Yama Rāja, the fearful and final judge of the dead. He rides his vehicle, the Bull, which represents animal passion, while his sister Yamī offers him a skull-bowl filled with blood. Yama Rāja executes the law of karma, making visible to the dead the totality of their past actions in the mirror of karma. He also represents human conscience.

ABBOT OF DUNGKAR GOMPA
Chumbi Valley

This abbot belongs to the Yellow Hat sect (Gelugpa) founded by Tsongkhapa, the fourteenth-century reformer. The Gelugpa sect attained temporal power over Tibet in the seventeenth century, and ruled the country from Lhasa. The Dalai Lama, who is the head of this sect, made Dungkar Gompa (the Monastery of the White Conch) his seat when he left Lhasa in flight from the Chinese invasion.

25

VILLAGE OF RUBIGANG
Tomo Valley, Southern Tibet

This village lies at the foot of the rocky hill on which Dung-kar Gompa (the Monastery of the White Conch) stands. One boy from this village, who was a *tulku*, lived at Dungkar Gompa. The village borders a level plain that is remarkable for its smooth, even surface. In this fertile valley, villagers grow wheat, for which reason the valley is called Wheat (Tomo) Valley.

A FROZEN WATERFALL AT DOTAK
Southern Tibet

The vast open skies of Tibet and the clarity of the atmosphere greatly increase one's appreciation of nature and its forces. This hundred-foot-high waterfall at Dotak (on the way to Gyantse) presented a breathtaking sight along the trek. It was completely frozen over. Contrary to what one might expect, the freezing begins at the bottom and moves gradually upward until the entire waterfall is a mass of solid ice.

MAITREYA BUDDHA OF
SANDO CHOLING GOMPA
Phari Dzong, Southern Tibet

This is an immense golden image of
Buddha Maitreya, which was housed in a
spacious gold and red painted hall at
Sando Choling Gompa at Phari. In accordance with traditional custom, the
image has been offered dozens of *khatas*, which hang from its hands. Each
thread in each *khata* represents a flower
in bloom. The altar was richly colored
and decorated, and on the table stood
tormas and cakes, and other customary
ritual offerings.

LAMA PRIEST OF SANDO CHOLING GOMPA
Phari Dzong

Before a *pūja* (devotional service) begins, everything is carefully inspected and checked. The offering table is stacked high with pastries, fruits, and other delicacies. Over these hang garlands of hardened cheese cubes. Milk is never drunk in Tibet, but is used for making hard cheese, pieces of which Tibetans love to suck for hours and hours, during long treks.

29

BUDDHAS OF THE PAST, PRESENT, AND FUTURE
Sando Choling Gompa, Phari Dzong

Buddha images such as these line both walls in the main hall of Sando Choling Monastery in Southern Tibet. Each image is shown seated on a golden lotus-throne, and is beautifully clothed in rich brocade robes. The forum of the hall is painted with representations of the Wheel of Life (which depicts the different stages through which life may pass). The low tables bearing Chinese symbols on them and the red and gold painted pillars add further magnificence to the awe-inspiring scene in this beautiful temple.

TIBETAN SIDDHA
THANG TONG GYALPO
Sando Choling Gompa

The *siddhās* were 'perfected ones' who attained direct realization by converting their weaknesses into strengths. They lived in India, primarily between the sixth and the tenth centuries, and in Tibet after Buddhism was established there. Many of the *siddhās*, like Thang Tong Gyalpo, reached perfection while continuing to work in the world. Thang Tong Gyalpo was a fifteenth-century ironsmith and a famous bridgebuilder, who introduced into Tibet bridges suspended from iron chains. He is therefore usually depicted with an iron chain in his hand.

TIBETAN MONK STUDYING SCRIPTURES
Phari Dzong

Monasteries in Tibet were traditionally places of study, and it was not uncommon to see novice lamas studying in a quiet corner of their rooms. The young monks spent many hours each day memorizing holy scriptures, *Sūtras*, and prayers. This one was fully absorbed in memorizing certain passages. The scriptures were printed by wood blocks (*parshing*) on rectangular pieces of daphne-bark paper.

CONTEMPLATING LAMA
Phari Dzong

In Tibet, religious practice is not reserved only for temples or shrines, but is a part of daily life. This picture shows a monk meditating in a monastery kitchen while the food is being cooked. Near him are Tibetan teacups with covers, on decorative stands. While watching the big cooking-urn of the monastery, this Lama had fallen into deep meditation.

LAMA SCHOLAR OF GANDEN
Rizong Pordoh Monastery,
Phari Dzong

He was the Dean of one of the philosophical faculties of the Monastic University of Ganden. Ganden Monastery,
which was founded in the early fifteenth
century, was one of the three major
Gelugpa monasteries near Lhasa. Each
of these monasteries had many branch
monasteries. This high Lama had been
invited to the branch monastery of Rizong Pordoh at Phari Dzong to teach
the little boy who was the reincarnation
of a famous abbot.

LAMA GOVINDA IN THE RED GORGE
Lhasa Route, Central Tibet

This narrow gorge, lined by natural rocky walls, was somewhat notorious for robberies. Travelers on foot were easily waylaid by bandits either on horseback or on foot. Even if a traveler were on horseback, he found it difficult to chase a mounted bandit, for bandits carried no luggage, and therefore traveled much faster than their pursuers.

TIBETAN PILGRIM
Central Tibet

This pilgrim carries his bedding and provisions on his back. For protection, he carries a staff with prayer flags on which sacred texts are inscribed. The prayer flags also indicate to other Tibetans that he is on a religious pilgrimage. Travel on foot was common in Tibet. No wheel was known to exist within Tibet except the prayer wheel, because of a prophesy that use of the wheel would destroy the social structure of the country. Travel was therefore on foot, or on riding animals such as mules, horses, or yaks.

A Religious Tibetan Pilgrim
Central Tibet

In order to receive alms from pious people, this pilgrim recites prayers to the accompaniment of bell and drum. In the bag near his right arm he carries *tsampa* (barley roasted whole and ground into flour), to eat along the way. *Tsampa* is the staple food of Tibet. Many such pilgrims were seen along the Lhasa route.

BROKEN ICE AT RHAM-TSO
Central Tibet

Lake Rham-Tso lies at an elevation of fifteen thousand feet
above sea level. It completely freezes over during winter. At
many places along the shore, the ice is broken by fierce winds,
and lies heaped into wild, fantastic shapes. This picture shows
forms resembling lotus leaves. The mountain range in the
background is the Central Himalayan Range, which forms the
border between Tibet and Bhutan.

ANCIENT WOODWORK IN THE TEMPLE OF KYANGPHU
Tsang Province, Central Tibet

Wooden structures are very rare in Tibet because trees grow only in protected valleys at lower altitudes, up to about twelve thousand feet. The wooden columns of this temple were brought from the Tsangpo Valley (about a fifteen-day journey by caravan) hundreds of years ago. The temple dates from the thirteenth century, at which time cedar trees were still growing in the Tsangpo Valley. The wood is notched and fitted together, for metal was thought to be so valuable that it was never used for nails. The bracketed structure that supports the ceiling is used all over Tibet, and is common in China and Japan as well.

TEMPTATION OF THE BUDDHA
Kyangphu Monastery, Central Tibet

The Buddha is depicted sitting in the niche of a *chorten* (a Buddhist monument derived from the *stūpa*). He is attacked by a host of demons led by Māra, the Evil One, who tries to turn him away from enlightenment, toward the world of illusion, samsara. In front of the *chorten* are white gauze scarves (*khatas*), which have been placed there by devotees as offerings and as marks of veneration.

A Buddha Image
Kyangphu Monastery

This thirteenth or fourteenth century image is probably a form of Vairocana, one of the five meditation or Dhyāni-Buddhas. These Buddhas, who never existed as historical figures, symbolize certain virtues and meditative experiences, and aid devotees in opening to their inner natures. Vairocana represents the original light of pure consciousness. This image, like many of the images at Kyangphu, shows a strong Indian influence. At the foot of the throne is a book of scriptures, wrapped in cloth. A votive lamp burns next to it.

41

Amitābha Buddha
Kyangphu Monastery

Amitābha is the Dhyāni-Buddha of Infinite Light. With the brilliant light of compassion and distinguishing wisdom that emanates from him, he enlightens countless sentient beings. He is shown here in his Sambhogakāya (Body of Bliss) form, in which he manifests to higher meditative states. His ornaments reveal his virtues to the devotee. His highly decorated throne is supported by two peacocks, the vehicles (or throne-animals) of Buddha Amitābha.

DHYĀNI-BUDDHA AMOGHASIDDHI
Kyangphu Monastery

The Dhyāni-Buddha Amoghasiddhi is the personification of unselfish, egoless action, the Wisdom that Accomplishes All Works. His right hand is raised in the *abhaya mudrā*, the gesture of fearlessness and of blessing. He is depicted here in his Sambhogakāya form, clad in rich garments and ornaments that denote his virtues.

43

DHYĀNI-BUDDHA VAIROCANA
Iwang Temple, Tsang Province

Dhyāni-Buddha Vairocana is the radiating Sun Buddha who sits in the center of the mandala, the pure sphere of consciousness. As he sits in meditation, he, like all other Dhyāni-Buddhas, sends innumerable Buddha-visions into the world to inspire others. The rows of metal images to either side (just behind him) form part of his halo, and represent Dhyāni-Buddhas. As usual, many *khatas* have been thrown on him by devotees. Butter lamps and water bowls stand at the foot of the throne. His robes suggest the influence of Chinese Turkestan.

AMITĀBHA BUDDHA
IN CENTRAL ASIAN STYLE
Iwang Temple

In the year 1270, Kublai Khan, Emperor of the great Mongol Empire, was converted to Buddhism by the abbot of the Sakya lamasery. After the abbot returned to Tibet and founded the Sakya dynasty, Central Asian influence became apparent in Tibetan sculpture. The quilted robes of this Buddha are reminiscent of Chinese Turkestan. This statue from one of the temples of Iwang is well over life-size.

45

BODHISATTVAS
Central Asian Style, Iwang Temple

Bodhisattvas are the Enlightenment-Beings who, out of great wisdom and compassion, have chosen to delay the attainment of unconditioned nirvana in order to work for the enlightenment of all sentient beings. The heavy quilted robes of these Dhyāni-Bodhisattvas show the influence of the Central Asian style.

STANDING BUDDHAS
Central Asian Style, Iwang Temple

These Dhyāni-Buddhas (or Dhyāni-Bodhisattvas), who are standing on either side of the Buddha Śākyamuni in the Iwang Temple, are clad in Indian costumes, with shawl-ends hanging over their arms. Iwang was situated on the caravan route to India, and was influenced by both Indian and Central Asian styles.

MĀRA'S HOST (LEFT SIDE WALL)
Iwang Temple

This is a part of Māra's Host, which covers two complete walls, from floor to ceiling, on either side of the seated Śākyamuni Buddha in the ancient temple of Iwang, in Central Tibet. This entire temple is dedicated to the theme of 'The Temptation of the Buddha'. This theme is popular all over Tibet and is depicted in frescoes, *thanka* paintings, and sculptures in innumerable monasteries and shrines.

BUDDHA ŚĀKYAMUNI
Iwang Temple

This image represents the historical Buddha Śākyamuni in the process of gaining enlightenment. His right hand is about to touch the ground, calling the Earth to bear witness to the many lives of renunciation that entitle him to sit on the sacred spot under the Bodhi Tree. Māra, the Evil One, contests his right to the sacred spot, and tries to tempt him to swerve from his goal of ultimate enlightenment for the welfare of all beings. Māra calls upon his host of demons, who attack the Buddha with weapons and missiles of various kinds. Both of the side walls of this temple are covered with molded demons and other creatures, in fantastic forms. In the foreground is Sayum, the goddess of the Earth, who verifies the Buddha's claim. This life-sized statue of Śākyamuni stands in one of the temples of Iwang. Its style is Indian.

49

MĀRA'S HOST (RIGHT SIDE WALL)
Iwang Temple

Many of the bodies show faces of wrathful beings on shoulders, bellies, chests, and thighs. The figures are painted in bright colors, and appear very lifelike. Like many of the sculptures in Tibet, these figures are made of molded clay. In the dry Tibetan climate, the clay hardens to a rock-like consistency that is very durable and long-lasting.

BUDDHA RELIEFS AT SAUGANG
Central Tibet

As one leaves the high mountains and enters the great central plains of Gyantse, many Buddhas carved in stone greet the caravan. These immense Buddha reliefs at Saugang stand like friends who welcome or bid farewell to all who come and go along the Lhasa route.

ENTRANCE TO THE MAIN TEMPLE
OF NENYING
Central Tibet

The woodwork of this temple is beautifully painted, like that of most temples in Tibet. The trellis-work of the upper story windows is similar to that of China. Since there was no glass in Tibet, windows were covered with cloth, usually a thick beige Chinese silk (called tussah silk), which is very durable and good to look at.

Nenying Monastery
Central Tibet

This is one of the oldest monasteries in Tsang Province of
Central Tibet. It originally belonged to the Nyingmapa sect,
but was later taken over by the Gelugpas. It was one of the seats
of Dorje Phagmo (the Diamond Sow), the great Abbotess who
was regarded as the incarnation of the goddess Vajravārāhī.
She was the highest female religious dignitary in Tibet. In the
foreground stand two *chortens*.

NENYING MONASTERY,
WITH WEATHERMAKER'S RETREAT
ON TOP OF A ROCKY MOUNTAIN
Central Tibet

The Weathermaker, whose function was to control the weather, was a magician appointed by the government. He was expected to ward off hailstorms, droughts, and similar disasters that could damage crops. If he failed to do this, he was immediately relieved of his post. Since the Weathermaker of Nenying had held this post for a considerable time, there was reason to believe he was successful in his work.

CHORTEN AT NENYING MONASTERY
Central Tibet

Chortens, religious monuments originally built as reliquaries, came to represent the universe in Buddhist cosmology. They symbolize the five elements of the universe: earth, water, fire, air, and ether. These elements are conceived as different states of density in a constantly materializing and dematerializing universe, and also as spiritual forces operating in the psychic centers of the human body and mind. On the hilltop in the background is the Weathermaker's retreat, sparkling against the bright blue Tibetan sky.

LAMA GOVINDA IN TIBET
Tsang Province, Central Tibet

He is reading in one of the rest houses along the route to Lhasa. At regular distances, about fifteen miles apart, Dak Bungalows or rest houses had been built for traveling officials or government-appointed travelers. Traveling was customary from dawn to noon, in order to avoid the piercing winter winds that rose after midday. In the cold season, fur caps, colored red or yellow, were sometimes worn by the lamas.

Lama Govinda Against The Weathermaker's Mountain Retreat
Nenying, Central Tibet

A story is told about weathermaking in Tibet. An area near Lhasa that had suffered from drought for seven years called in a weathermaker. A visitor saw the officiating monks chanting scriptures from the Prajñāpāramitā (the sacred scripture of Mahāyāna Buddhism), and wondered how a text that had nothing to do with rain could have an influence upon the weather. But by the time he had returned to his quarters, it suddenly began to rain so heavily that all the streets were filled with water.

57

PALACE OF THE GOVERNOR OF GYANTSE
Gyantse, Central Tibet

Yabshi Phunkhang was the residence of the Governor of Gyantse, a relative of the Mahārāja of Sikkim. It was given to us during our stay in Gyantse. It contained many rooms with frescoed walls, and a large and spacious compound with a garden. The trees along the right are poplars.

DECORATIVE BALCONIES OF YABSHI PHUNKHANG
Gyantse

This picture shows the beautiful brightly painted and carved woodwork that was characteristic of all good homes in Tibet, especially homes of the nobility in Gyantse, Lhasa, and other cities. Gyantse, with a population of about fifty thousand, was the second largest city in Tibet, and the most important trading center with India.

ENTRANCE OF A MONASTERY
Gyantse

Lama Govinda is going up the steps to the domicile ot the
Lhabrangtse, the Gelugpa monk-official who was appointed
by the government to be the Governor of the Monastic City
of Gyantse. There were about sixteen different monasteries
in this monastic city.

INTERIOR OF A TIBETAN HOME
Gyantse

Tibetan homes were usually decorated with *thankas* (religious scrolls) and lucky signs (religious symbols). The walls, pillars, and woodwork were generally painted in bright colors. In the best room of the house there was found a shrine with seven water bowls and one or more butter lamps as offerings. The hard cushion-seats, which were used for sitting on during the day, were folded out to form beds at night. Low wooden tables (*choktses*) were used for tea and snacks, and for meals.

TSANG PROVINCE HEADDRESS
Tsang Province, Central Tibet

This is the traditional headdress of the women of Tsang Province in Central Tibet. Unlike the women of Lhasa, who wear their hair loose and flowing, these women braid their hair into one hundred and eight thin, tiny plaits. (One hundred and eight is a sacred number.) Ü and Tsang were regarded as the heart of Tibet and called Ü-Tsang, the central provinces.

WOMEN OF SAUGANG IN TSANG PROVINCE HEADDRESS
Central Tibet

After joining the plaits to end in two long plaits below their
shoulders, the women of Tsang Province complete the headdress by fixing the tiny plaits to a light cloth-covered frame
richly decorated with seed pearls and coral and turquoise
stones. The higher the woman's station in life, the larger the
stones in her jewelry and headdress. Silver and gold ornaments
were also worn.

LADY OF LHASA
Gyantse

Among the well-to-do Tibetans, women's dress and coiffure were very prominent. Hair-styles varied from province to province, but Lhasa, the capital, always set the style in dress. Aprons, *chupas*—coat-dresses made of satin brocade with or without gold—and jewelry ran into fabulous sums. Charm-boxes studded with turquoise and coral and hung from the neck were the most important ornaments. The earrings were almost always fashioned with enormous blue turquoise stones arranged in traditional patterns; because of their weight, they were hung from a loop around the ear or suspended from the headdress frame. This picture shows a noble-woman of Lhasa in the local style and dress. The crescent-shaped frame, decorated with coral and pearl, is fixed to the top of the head. Her long, loose hair is then combed to the front and made to fall in cascades down to the shoulders.

LADIES OF GYANTSE
Central Tibet

The ladies in this picture are the wives of officials who worked in the Indo-Tibetan Trade Mission, which was housed in a special fort outside of Gyantse. The colorfully striped woolen aprons worn by the women in Tibet were woven in strips about ten inches wide, and then sewn together in such a way that the stripes, deliberately unmatched, formed a special design. The aprons of wealthier women had brocaded corners and were made of wool so finely woven that they were more expensive than silk.

A LADY OF LHASA WITH HER ATTENDANTS
Gyantse

Noblewomen and noblemen of Tibet liked to be photographed with their attendants, for having numerous servants was a mark of nobility. Since there was never any exact census in Tibet, the precise proportion of the Tibetan nobility, or the size of any class within the society was unknown. Note the difference in the headdress worn by this lady from Lhasa and the headdress worn by the ladies of Tsang Province.

CHANG-BEARERS IN A TIBETAN PLAY
Gyantse

Chang is the name for Tibetan beer, which is made from fermented barley. These *chang*-bearers in one of the religious dramas at Gyantse served the *chang* from large urns such as that held by the woman on the right. *Chang* was a common drink in Tibet and served as a digestive ingredient in the otherwise starchy Tibetan food. If taken in great quantities, it was moderately intoxicating.

TIBETAN FISHERMAN IN A JĀTAKA PLAY
Gyantse

Jātaka tales are stories of the former lives of Buddha Śākyamuni. Dramatic presentations of these stories were enacted in monasteries and courtyards of rich people all over Tibet. During performances, the audience, which at times totaled hundreds, would sit or stand on the verandahs and balconies surrounding the courtyard. The mask shown here depicts a fisherman. Since fishing and hunting were regarded in Tibet as a violation of the Buddhist faith, the occupation of a fisherman was considered to be one of the very lowest.

JĀTAKA PLAY
Gyantse

In the larger monasteries, religious plays could last for two or three days. Far-off villagers would walk great distances to see them, spending the night in the outhouses of the monastery or camping in its vicinity. These were special celebrations to be enjoyed to the fullest. Sometimes brocaded costumes worth fabulous sums were worn by the actors. All costumes and accessories were the property of the monastery. Women's parts were played by young men or boys, never by women.

A NUN WITH HER MOTHER
Central Tibet

The nun seen in the picture was the daughter of the lady to the right. Monks and nuns were better educated than the average layman, and were highly respected and venerated. Nuns were sometimes known as scholars who could be consulted in various matters; some became heads of monasteries. Non-incarnated nuns could also rise to high positions. An example is the well-known Abbotess of a Nyingma monastery near Lhasa, who was regarded as one of the most learned and holy persons in Tibet.

STUDYING THE SCRIPTURES
Gyantse

Students work on low tables and warm themselves under the strong rays of the sun in an open verandah. Through years of memorizing sacred scriptures, monks became great repositories of the Dharma. Absorbing texts for oral reproduction was considered far more valuable than owning a vast library, especially during discussions, when recalling passages could deepen awareness and understanding. Only after a student had mastered the teachings was he encouraged to write or teach.

71

CHORTEN AT THE FOOT OF GYANTSE FORT
Central Tibet

The original Big Fort of Gyantse was situated on a rocky spur, outside of the town proper. It looked very impressive, although it had been partially destroyed by British artillery during the Tibetan campaign of 1904 (which enforced the granting of British trading posts at Ya-tung, Gyantse, and Gartok). Only a few religious buildings had been left intact in the Fort, and it was no longer inhabited. The *chorten*, symbol of the Buddha, as well as that of the universe, is a reminder of the transience of everything made up of the five elements, including life itself.

GELUGPA MONASTERY
Gyantse

This is one of the Gelugpa monasteries in the Monastic City of Gyantse, surmounted by the building on which the main temple's immense *thanka* of appliqué-work was displayed once a year. The doctrinal system of the Gelugpa sect was defined by Tsongkhapa in the fifteenth century as emphasizing the 'Middle Path' (Mādhyamika), the doctrines of the perfection of knowledge (Prajñāpāramitā), and increasing attention to monastic discipline. This sect held political power in Tibet.

MONASTERIES OF GYANTSE
Central Tibet

Gyantse was divided into two parts—the secular town and the monastic city (shown in this picture), which was surrounded by walls that followed the contours of the hills around it. The Monastic City of Gyantse contained monasteries of all the different schools of Tibetan Buddhism. Lama dignitaries and other religious persons who came to Gyantse stayed in their respective lamaseries in this monastic town. In the center is the main temple (Tsug Lhakhang), which could seat a thousand monks in its great hall, one of the largest in Tibet. Next to it is the great nine-storied Golden *Chorten* of the "Hundred Thousand Images' (Kumbum). The square, stone building on top of the city-wall was used for displaying the main temple's enormous, appliqué-work *thanka* (temple banner) on special occasions. This could be seen for many miles around.

Assembly Hall Of The Main Temple Of Gyantse
Central Tibet

The padded seats in the big hall of this temple were used by the one thousand monks who took part in the services. Because of its great spaciousness, this temple has been called the Cathedral of Gyantse. Its pillars were painted with beautiful red lacquer, and all of the capitals were elaborately carved and brightly colored.

KUMBUM, THE TEMPLE OF THE HUNDRED THOUSAND IMAGES
Gyantse

The architecture of the Gyantse Kumbum (which is similar to that of the original plan of the Borobudur of Java) is based on the mandala, a concentric design used in meditation, and combines the form of the *chorten* with the elements of a temple. The Kumbum contained eighty separate chapels, which were arranged around the center of the mandala according to their function and importance. Each chapel was frescoed from the ceiling to the ground, and contained numerous sculptures and images of Buddhist deities. The drum-like, circular portion in the middle housed four large chapels dedicated to the four Dhyāni-Buddhas, each of which governed a world quarter of the mandala. The presiding Buddha stood in a separate chapel on the very top of the golden-ridged roof.

THE KUMBUM FROM ABOVE
Gyantse

As the devotee entered the precincts of the Mandala-Temple, he considered himself at the beginning of a great spiritual journey. Each chapel was dedicated to a particular aspect of Buddha or Bodhisattvahood and had its own particular form of worship and meditative practice. The central figure in each chapel was surrounded by its emanations and attributes of power in the form of sculptures and frescoes that covered every wall from the ceiling to the ground. The spiritual forces of these innumerable enlightened beings helped and inspired the devotee, and revealed to him the infinite possibilities of realization. As he ascended from plane to plane, and circumambulated terrace after terrace, concentrating on every step he took, the devotee brought before his mind's eye the various stages of realization. With each story he ascended, he reached a higher plane of intuitive wisdom. At the very top, all diversity disappeared, and the devotee was confronted with the ultimate integration of wisdom and compassion, mind and heart, feeling and knowledge, in the symbol of Dorje Chang, the pure original consciousness who here functionally corresponded to the Adi-Buddha, the primordial Buddha who resides in the very center of every being.

DHYĀNI-BUDDHA VAIROCANA
Gyantse Kumbum

The Dhyāni-Buddha Vairocana, the Spiritual Sun Buddha, occupies the center of the Kumbum mandala. He is the sum total of the four outer Dhyāni-Buddhas, the embodiment of the pure sphere of consciousness. His color is usually white (in this case blue), and his gesture is that of Turning the Wheel of the Universal Law (*dharmacakra pravartana mudrā*).

Dhyāni-Buddha Ratnasambhava
Gyantse Kumbum

This two-story-high statue of Dhyāni-Buddha Ratnasambhava stood in the Southern shrine room of the Kumbum. His body is golden; his complexion, yellow. His gesture of giving (*dāna mudrā*) expresses the wisdom of the essential equality of all beings. His necklaces, earrings, and other ornaments represent virtues and accomplishments seen in his Body of Inspiration (Sambhogakāya). His emblem is the three-fold jewel (not seen in this picture). In Tibet, all ornaments placed on Buddhas, Bodhisattvas, saints, and realized beings were made of gold and silver and precious or semi-precious stones, for nothing but the very best was ever given to the enlightened ones.

79

DHYĀNI-BUDDHA AMITĀBHA
Gyantse Kumbum

Buddha Amitābha is the Buddha of Infinite Light. He is of red complexion, and his position in the mandala of meditation is in the West, in the place of the setting sun. His *mudrā* is that of meditation, with his hands in his lap, the right hand resting over the left palm. His rich adornments signify that he is in the inspirational body (Sambhogakāya), in which he displays all the virtues and blissful joys experienced in meditation. This gigantic image, two stories high, stood in the Western shrine room of the Temple of the Hundred Thousand Images in Gyantse, Central Tibet.

HEAD OF DHYĀNI-BUDDHA RATNASAMBHAVA
Gyantse Kumbum

This picture was taken from a tiny sky-light on the second story, facing the head. His five-pointed crown, like those of all the Dhyāni-Buddhas, represents the Five Wisdoms that are realized in meditation: the Wisdom of the Great Mirror (mirrorlike wisdom), the Wisdom of Essential Equality, the Distinguishing Wisdom, the Wisdom of Self-less Activity, and the Transcendental Wisdom of the Dharma realm.

IMAGE OF BUDDHA ŚĀKYAMUNI
Gyantse Kumbum

Buddha Śākyamuni is the historical Buddha of our era. Here he is shown in the gesture of touching the earth (*bhūmisparśa mudrā*), which he used when challenged by Māra, just before his enlightenment. By this gesture he called Sayum, goddess of the earth, as witness to his spiritual accomplishments in this, as well as his previous births. These accomplishments entitled him to occupy the seat under the Tree of Enlightenment, or as it was later called, the Diamond Throne (*vajrāsana*).

82

DHYĀNI-BUDDHA AMOGHASIDDHI
Gyantse Kumbum

He is the Buddha of the Northern shrine room of the meditation mandala. His color is blue-green and his *mudrā* is that of blessing and fearlessness. He is the embodiment of the Wisdom that Accomplishes All Works. The double-crossed *vajra* (Scepter of Spiritual Power) on his right palm signifies the universality of his power. The north also represents midnight, the time of the hidden ripening of spiritual activity.

83

YUMCHENMO PRAJÑĀPĀRAMITĀ
Gyantse Kumbum

Yumchenmo is the Great Mother of the Transcendental Wisdom, and the embodiment of the sacred scriptures of Mahāyāna Buddhism, Prajñāpāramitā. The highest form of Dolma or Tārā in Tibet, she is regarded as the Mother of all the Buddhas. She has four arms. The two hands before her breasts are in the gesture of Setting in Motion the Wheel of the Universal Law, which was proclaimed by the Buddha of our age (the historical Buddha Śākyamuni), in the Deer Park of Rṣipatana, near Benares. Her two other hands hold a *vajra* (not shown in this picture), and the sacred book of Transcendental Knowledge.

84

AMITĀBHA BUDDHA
IN DHYĀNA MUDRĀ
Gyantse Kumbum

Amitābha is the Dhyāni-Buddha of Infinite Light. His *mudrā* is that of meditation, with the hands in the lap, the right hand placed over the left palm. Here he is shown in his Sambhogakāya form, with a robe and jewelry that symbolize his virtues. His body is red, and his ornaments golden. His heavenly realm is the Western Paradise, where he resides in infinite splendor among the enlightened.

AVALOKITEŚVARA
Gyantse Kumbum

This is a form of Avalokiteśvara, the great Bodhisattva of compassion and mercy, recognized by the deerskin over his left shoulder. (The deer symbolizes compassion.) He is two-armed and his right hand is in the *mudrā* of giving. In Tibet he is known as Chenrezig. Avalokiteśvara is regarded as the active emanation of Amitābha Buddha, the Buddha of Infinite Light. Amitābha gave him the task of working for the good of all creatures.

Jowo Rimpoche—The Crowned Buddha Śākyamuni As Prince
Gyantse

This is the main image in the great Assembly Hall of the main temple of the Monastic City of Gyantse. It was said to be a copy of the statue of Jowo Rimpoche brought to Tibet from China in the seventh century by the Chinese wife of Srongtsen Gampo. The original sculpture was housed in the main temple in Lhasa.

87

THE GREEN TĀRĀ
Gyantse Kumbum

She is one of the most important of the twenty-one aspects of Tārā, the Madonna of Tibetan Buddhism. She is said to be born from a tear of compassion shed by Avalokiteśvara when he looked down on the world and saw its suffering. She is very popular, for she is the protectress of all who are in distress, and is believed to protect travelers in particular. Her right hand is stretched out in the gesture of giving, while the left holds the stem of a lotus flower with a gesture of blessing. She sits on a lotus with her right leg on the ground, as if rising to help all suffering beings who pray to her. Her color is green, like that of Amoghasiddhi (the Accomplisher of All Selfless Acts), who is her counterpart. This image stood in one of the eighty chapels in the famous Gyantse Kumbum.

VAJRASATTVA
Gyantse Kumbum

Vajrasattva is one of the Dhyāni-Bodhisattvas (the active emanation of transcendental Buddhahood visualized in meditation). The name Vajrasattva means the Diamond Being, i.e. the very nature of our immortal mind, which is hidden beneath the veil of our mundane consciousness and the illusion of ego-hood. He is the principle of our original purity, which is restored in the moment of enlightenment. In his hands he holds the Diamond Scepter of Spiritual Power (*vajra*), which symbolizes active compassion, and the ritual Bell (*ghaṇṭa*), which symbolizes wisdom. Enlightenment can be attained only when knowledge is combined with compassion and love.

89

DHARMAVIJĀYA
Gyantse Kumbum

Dharmavijāya represents the victory of the Dharma, the universal and moral law preached by the Buddha, over the forces of darkness and ignorance that try to prevent ultimate liberation. She is shown here in her Sambhogakāya form, with three heads and six arms, wearing robes and jewelry that symbolize her virtues.

YUMCHENMO
Gyantse Kumbum

This view of Yumchenmo shows the *vajra* held in one of her right hands. This beautiful gilt statue, made of molded, sun-dried clay (like most of the statues in the Kumbum), is much over life-size. The gilding gives it a wonderful warm glow. Yumchenmo is the embodiment of Prajñāpāramitā, the highest Transcendental Wisdom.

Mañjughoṣa Sinhanāda
Gyantse Kumbum

The Bodhisattva Mañjughoṣa Sinhanāda is here proclaiming the Dharma to the world with the voice of a lion, his hands in the gesture of Turning the Wheel of the Universal Law. He stretches out his left foot as if to dismount from the roaring lion, for he is ready to help all suffering beings. He is orange-red in color.

ATTENDANT BODHISATTVA
Gyantse Kumbum

The Buddha is often shown attended by the Vedic gods Śākra and Indra. In this case, his attendants are two Bodhisattvas, one of which is shown here: Grace and Beauty personified.

93

PROTECTOR OF THE LAW
Gyantse Kumbum

This Defender of the Religious Law has three faces and six arms. His body is dark blue in color; his three faces are white, blue, and red. He wears a human skin around his shoulders. A devotee with offerings stands next to him.

MILAREPA, THE POET-SAINT OF TIBET
Gyantse Kumbum

Milarepa is perhaps the most beloved of all Tibetan saints. He was both a yogi and a poet, a singer of many songs. In this picture he is shown with the left hand between the ear and the mouth, a gesture that expresses the act of singing. In his right hand he holds a horn in which he kept salt; this horn and an earthen pot were his only possessions. He was the pupil of Marpa, the founder of the Kargyud School, and is famous through his biography and his *Hundred Thousand Songs*, which popularized Buddhist thought. He lived in the twelfth century.

GROUP FROM THE SIXTEEN STHĀVIRAS
Gyantse Kumbum

According to tradition, Sthāviras or elders were the direct disciples of the Buddha Śākyamuni. Originally there were sixteen foremost disciples who were entrusted by Śākyamuni Buddha with the preservation of his teachings. They wandered all over northern India to spread these teachings. One whole temple-hall in the Kumbum is dedicated to these sixteen disciples. This picture shows six of them. There is a remarkable similarity between these sculptures and the images of saints in medieval cathedrals.

KINGS OF TIBET
Gyantse Kumbum

Srongtsen Gampo, Tisong Detsen, and Ralpachan were the three great religious kings of Tibet, the foremost promoters of Buddhism, who ruled during the period from the seventh to the ninth centuries. This picture shows Srongtsen Gampo (left) and Tisong Detsen. Among his many achievements, Srongtsen Gampo commissioned the devising of a Tibetan alphabet suitable for translating Buddhist works, and instituted a general code of conduct which served to prepare his subjects for the practice of the Buddhist religion. In the eighth century, Tisong Detsen invited the Indian Bodhisattvas Padmasambhava and Śāntarakṣita to Tibet, and thus planted the Buddhist tradition in his country. During his reign, Samye monastery, the first center of Buddhist learning in Tibet, was established, many texts were translated, and numerous meditation centers founded.

DECORATIVE DOOR FRAME
Gyantse Kumbum

In Tibet there is hardly any religious architecture that does
not display colorful decorations. This door frame is at the
entrance of one of the temples of the Kumbum. The lion-
headed Garuḍa (whose head is usually shown as that of an
eagle) is holding his natural enemy, the snake, in his mouth.
Eagle-headed Garuḍas are often shown over images of Buddhas
as symbols of protection.

98

CHUMITANG NUNNERY
Central Tibet

This nunnery stands deep in the folds of the mountains, near
Gyantse. The big buildings were used for assemblies and the
smaller ones for living quarters. One member of every Tibetan
family was generally given over to the religion, to become
either a monk or a nun.